EIGHT

2

TWO

Sasha Newborn

MUDBORN PRESS   2013

Eight 2 Two
copyright © 2013 Mudborn Press
ISBN 978-0-930012-60-1

MUDBORN PRESS

First Person Intense   The Basement   Eight 2 Two

Italian for Opera Lovers. (dictionary)   French for Food Lovers

BANDANNA BOOKS

Don't Panic: The Procrastinator's Guide to Writing an Effective Term Paper.
The First Detective: 3 Stories. Edgar Allan Poe   Gandhi on the *Bhagavad Gita*
The Everlasting Gospel, William Blake   Frankenstein, Mary Shelley
Dante and His Circle. Love sonnets   Vita Nuova, Dante on Beatrice
Ghazals of Ghalib   The Gospel According to Tolstoy
                Hadji Murad, a Chechen story, Leo Tolstoy
Mitos y Leyendas/Myths and Legends of Mexico. Bilingual
The Beechers Through the 19th Century
Uncle Tom's Cabin, H.B. Stowe   Aurora Leigh, E.B. Browning

TEACHING SUPPLEMENTS

(Q and A, glossaries, critical comments)
Areopagitica, John Milton   Apology of Socrates & The Crito, Plato
Leaves of Grass, Walt Whitman   Sappho, The Poems
Uncle Tom's Cabin, Harriet Beecher Stowe

SHAKESPEARE FOR DIRECTORS, PRODUCERS, ACTORS, WANNABEES

DIRECTOR'S PLAYBOOK SERIES. the elements of production: storyboarding,
auditions, staging diagrams, budget, publicity, costuming, set design, playbill,
                stage managing, glossary, customized actor scripts

Hamlet   The Merchant of Venice   Twelfth Night   Taming of the Shrew
A Midsummer Night's Dream   Romeo and Juliet   As You Like It   Richard III
Henry V   Much Ado About Nothing   Macbeth   Othello

plus
7 Plays with Transgender Characters   Falstaff: Four Plays   Venus and Adonis

*F*oreword

Eight 2 *Two*, poems from the Seventies and onward, is a compilation of short poems by a declared "non-poet." The title, likewise, demonstrates a different way of looking at something familiar. In case you haven't figured it out, the explanation is at the end of the book.

My personal opinion on poetry is that it is more important for the poet to write than it is for the reader to read. You be the judge.

Birdie Newborn
February 2013

Contents

to the good years

8

How to read
              leap
                    there's no
stopping only the flow there's
now & that must be enough
there's now
                    & there's memories
you are the lense you are the
echo chamber the seashell
through whose chambers all sounds
come together like waves

18

this may all be a mistake
but it's *my* mistake
and I'll probably
keep making it
until I die.

80

…a peaceful river.
On the way to waking
troubled dreams tumble
across our vision,
smoky embers suffocate the air,
a clean horizon boiling out and
blown abroad.
Hudson's crew saw landfall in
a narrow bay, a pretty place,
a doorway to a dream, a promise.
The flow has never stanched,
white sails gone, bridges arch
over the water.

88

There's a voice in me that says
  wake up
      your life is half over
          the best part is yet to come
          if only you'd
              wake up

Words equipotential non-sequential a torrent:
…I uttered my own name from my own mouth and
Korea" to stop them and we did not need to worry about
       getting the US
lege tamen certa: si nullos contigit illic
Hélène was leaving 27 rue de Fleurus because, her hus-
from her arms how far she wanted to go. "Listen to
And then that is is broken…. and then it reappears.
a flight of empurpled wings!
where they flee. Now that the war is centralized in this
hangman's knot—on the bus from the air terminal a

84

There are corners I still hide in
lights I can't look at,
people I can't describe
—& thru it all
I say to myself:
                    You are not alone.
I write my pieces in that dark brilliance
the late afternoon sun slanting thru the small
        window,
books piled in one corner, papers in another.
                    Whatever is to be done,
                    I will have to do it now.

89

awful when hope
ardry wet cull
olly way call
ony were quill
only wart quail
orderly war trial
wardery ort royal
walletry port rail
wilery portrayal
wil try pontrail
wintry pen rail

81

peace human peace is not forever,
only the child may sleep, only the innocent
& none of us are innocent—
our faces tell it and the words out of our mouths.
peace—a mask a smile pasted on,
nobody asked for this peace
we are numb
        we are a dream and the beast of a dream

87

wild child
tonight, child,
tonight under the stars

86

a good page
is lost
every minute.

𝟾𝟹

    Sick day:
Graham cracker
potato chips—big
tuna—chunk light
beer
milk
cigarettes
Cadbury mint bar or
    semi-sweet (Ghirardelli)
    chocolate
saltines

82

When I Sing

When I sing
I sing for you
The many wonders of the earth
              are floating all around,
and I can count the stars
              a-gleaming in your eyes.
I see apples in the smile you cannot hide.

I see dancing in your fingers
and deep   clean   breath,
and there's everlasting joy in your heart
and there's room for everybody in your heart.

11

Don Juan on the beach
is not on this beach
this
slow earth oscillation of waves
builds with the weight of the push,
draws down
the long wash I walk through.
I am not Don Juan
but I can't forget his beach
or Odysseus beached—naked   alive
burned by the sun the hot sand the sweat.
I am cool, walking, my feet clean after the foam
        recedes,
tiny splashes the thousand suns on wet sand
        catch me
this is my beach

15

I gather strength from frogs like word charms
I stand at the bridge, I look up I listen
They are strong they make the voice of the creek
come alive I hear echoes off the concrete walls
They are many they are one I am one
I am one I speak
                  with a pen
I am many we are the poem
this night

50

Chris, seventy-one and drunk without his teeth
says he threw away Rosie's leash when
it broke. Old Rosie with the dangling wattle
waddles out into the fast one-way,
 & Chris resolutely steps out to protect her—
four cars slow to a stop—thank god this is California
—but Chris almost tips himself over at the far curb—
I think the leash was for him

                        as much as for Rosie

58

Not lying is the first step
to saying the truth

55

I throw my passion
into words
they are not big enough
I am shrinking

Nostalgia only in the cosmic sense,
remembering what we never knew.
Sesshu

(Gesundheit)

59

I kissed the mirror tonight
—perhaps I should take a backward leap

like the Chinese painters who travel far
without brush,
then come back to their studios
to paint what they had seen.

51

When even the cricket stops its song
we all pause,
we pass through a space in summer
between two words.
Memories of another continent
flock around a formless
idea of cricket-silence, ssh
krrrp krrrp I hear it 4/4,
 & when they stop, I hear
more than crickets or silence
it's not 4/4, it's snakelike
inside my head from ear to ear
constant

In the quiet
after sex,
I hear traffic,
a prop-driven airplane.
The wind bellies in
the curtain, cooling
our thin sweat.
After these million years,
we get no closer than this.

56

I've eaten shit in my life.

53

It's
as if we've been here before
but hadn't firmly grasped
this moment
enough
to make it last.

52

Sometimes I see myself
surrounded by friends
slightly drunk
& having a good time.
sometimes I feel like a stranger
speaking to myself in a language
no one has heard of,
& I'm looking at the same faces
& grinning,
waiting for a nod,
a wink, a grin.

5

I go to my room
seeking quietness,
to be as empty as the air—
with the sounds of a washing machine
someone watering a lawn,
a car turning a corner
a bird—
the sounds on my eardrums
when I'm not busy being me

40

To say the simplest things
I require strenuous language

48

the sugar demon strikes—
has his way, and then is gone.
I lie back, exhausted.
What was said?
What does this silence mask?
Cells burst.
My breath, heavy, falls to the ground
on top of the mountain of myself.
I get dizzy.
What am I hungry for?
I am loved, respected, complimented.
Why is that not enough?
Not enough. Not enough.
Life is not enough.

45

Savor by Pablo Neruda
translated by Sasha Newborn

Out of false chartings, from habits grown ridiculous,
spilling out endlessly and always carried alongside me,
I've saved one tendency, a solitary savor

Out of conversations as worn as used wood
with the humility of chairs, with words busy
serving as slaves of someone else's will,
it takes on that consistency of milk, of dead time,
of air trapped over cities.

Who can brag of a patience more solid?
Prudence wraps me in a tight skin,
its color blended like a snake's:
my babies come out of deep convulsions.
Oh, with one drink I can wave away this day
which I chose, the same as with all the days of the
        earth.

I live full of a dirt-colored substance, as silent
as an old mother, with a patience as certain
as a church's shadow or the sleep of bones.
I am filled by those deeply placed waters,
ready—nodding but sadly alert.

In my guitar insides, an old song plays,
dry and resonant, always present, always the same,
like a well-balanced meal, like smoke:
a lean bird guards my head:
in my steady knife lives an angel.

44

Breaking the Cup

There's no two ways about it,
the woman I'm with has got to be equal
or it isn't any good—
it's got to be 50-50.
Or, like David says,
maybe some nights it's 35-65
or other nights it's me & you,
 you & me, me & you, you
& me, we have to work it out
so all the chips don't slide down to one end,
so all the dishes get done
& two are doing it, not one,
not all the time, not for more than
a month or so—
somebody's got to complain,
somebody's got to yell or go out late &
screw around or
break the cup—
it's got to be equal,
one on one,
me & you,
you & me.

49

The Driving Mandala

toward an unknown proof
toward death
we drive ourselves forward
time licks at our elbows
we drive facing life
we push, hurrying time
& space is cramped
into our backpacks, suitcases
and time is encapsulated,
stuffed into our food.
we drive ourselves,
it is the highway Mahayana
Great Vehicle our normal
selves driving
falling forward
leaping from lane to lane
the freeway going
home.

41

the tastes of my life come in periods,
they're balanced or rounded out like a good meal
& now I must eat
                    & now I must suffer
                                        & now I must fuck
these are the time marks of depth, these free me
once I *know* the thorough flavor of a place-time-
        personality
& wish to change, like musical chairs
until the last go-around I die
and that I sometimes think
will be the best of all
the final submerging freezing letting go
                                        & whether
it will be pain or not
I look at death as fitting

47

And with suddenness, it comes
right there, full-blown
putting the nose right up against it,
so you don't see anything else

46

Only talking monkeys would invent telephones

Talk to me.
I can see you through the mists of my eyes
you vanish from right in front of me,
right where I thought you were.
I feel huge
and small, you're across a canyon.
But we talk.

42

Suspicions—
but always the big question, it becomes a howl
        —WHY?
yes this is all parenthesis
all a yearning yes those were better times
I'm convinced of this &
I want to know
who robbed the joy

4

I always start with me
that little hard knot
that point around which my stories swing

14

He's become gray,
he's fading out.
I know it.
He's getting ready to go,
saw his wife go,
her body, her heart just quit working
& he's probably wondering
with the arthritis in his leg
& the aches in the morning.
What's going to blow the fuse?
What pipe's going to burst?
What connection will break first?
There's no if any more,
there's only when.

9

One sup on a dime
ladle rat rotten hut
win two seeker grain mutter
adder how sin though hoods...

19

Some poems are never written

90

Say goodbye to yesterday, all those days
we didn't do enough, tired days
of eating & sleeping & fucking,
spaced-out by the inability
to say *I love you* enough,
give enough kisses to this shared life.

98

Life is a breakfast hastily swallowed
a breath of air
an answer
sparkling with throwaway lines

95

As I doze off late at night, grammar creaking,
literature attacking me on my very desk,
this solid wood shaking with vibrations
from the machine pounding in front of me—
this *voice* has an outlet, inside, a secret
that even I did not know.
But I trust the voice.

Remembering is not the process
by which this voice can be heard,
only by listening, listening, listening,
and not hearing anything else but
the voice coming out.

94

A life should be poetry,
so strongly itself
that you can smell it
like you can smell
a eucalyptus tree
from across the street.

99

By god, there are existential moments.
Spotty perceptions of my own reality,
my own body & what it touches,
what touches it/me—
yes, making that repulsive connection
that is really a recognition
that my mind is my body,
is my life.
I can't continue
thinking or believing it
and also believe in
mathematics or law or philosophy.

91

There's no going back, there's only going forward—
but if I could only
be aware of that all the time.
And not afraid. Not afraid.
To see, and then to do nothing—no, it's impossible,
this bourgeois numbness I am in,
it will fall of its own weight.
Clouds move, flowers bloom, I am alive—
even here by a lifeless machine,
the radio playing music a hundred years dead.

97

When I'm stoned, I remember:
how painful the truth is.
Those spots have worn so thin,
which is why I never look
at my own badness,
where I know I've been bad
and enjoy that,
even enjoy the twist of the pain.

96

The more I think of death and the shortness of life,
the more I steep myself in that urgency,
all the pettinesses fall away,
everything that I do matters,
every word I write—
nothing is written now for the sake of writing
or fame,
poor fame, as false as the glitter
of a polished abalone shell, which the abalone
never sees & never could see.
I write to keep tabs on a headlong rush
through time called my life.
That urgency.

93

The foxtails in the lot—
their most insistent quality
is the quality of life:
duplication.
Over and over.

92

The trick with words, so unlike
color on a palette,
the words must reflect a reality—
and the art is no art at all.

Poets—every poet I've known
had no choice in the matter.

1

I begin to think of these writings as reports on a life,
& try as I do, there'll always be more message
in the saying than the said.

100

I write also for my children I do not have
may never have
and can see this is my sureness
developing nicely into personality:
the childless father
the end of the line
the jumping off place
of this family gene repetition
the final word—
and into this word I go
submerged here into word-reality.

someday
I will be no other.

7

No matter how
I arrange my self
or my life,
something is
left out that,
sooner or later,
I have to deal with.

17

I only see them at parties
I only hear the news
when it's old
We keep in touch but never say
what's on our minds
except briefly
in the dark
drunk
between songs
and jokes.
I watch Bruce tilt up the
half-full samovar of punch
to show off his muscles,
his hands like Bill's sandcast of
hands hanging on the porch wall,

strong & reaching—
dance with the sweet-looking girl
                              who's by herself—
finally she smiles & loosens up
& when Jerry takes a break
from the congas,
he sweeps her away to the porch & the stars
& I make a new resolve,
seeing Bill's progress,
Bruce's arm,
Jerry's energy
to come back one more year,
& tell them what I really think & feel
& hug them
the next time I see them.

70

I lust in my heart
for a drop
of that satisfaction
that fucking can touch,
a moment of relief—
and how few of them.
My room now is
cold to the eye,
blank walls
that refuse to yield
their visions.
I am in a house
floating above history.

There are penalties
for indifference.

78

I have the image before me always of a book,
a physical book that may be opened—
that in it are contained
words and pictures—
but especially the pictures and
the insistent drone of the words
like someone talking
all the time.

Years later, I heard a voice—
the voice that must have been there
for a long time before that,
but now the voice had words—
and I was launched into the human trip.
Forever now the memory
of having been a child-animal
is in a scarcely readable language
—because of the words.

What is left of that world I once swam in?

75

A weinie or how I learned to tell my ass from a hole in
the ground:
how come she's wet when I'm hot but not not, not not,
but anyway I stuck it in her tired I wanted movement the
hips to do their things we could go to sleep
she said it hurt a little it was uncomfortable
I said oh she said well I pulled it out she said I'm sorry
I said it's all right & it was I didn't care any more
I rolled over said would she like to finish me she had her
hand on my chest she misunderstood I said never mind
let's sleep I'll do it myself I touched my cock
it was semi-hard still wet from inside her I held it
squeezed it like someone else's a piece of meat I let go
it took a while to go soft it always does after a good fuck
I don't remember my dreams but I had an appointment
with the bad guy I would have to come to terms & free
the child we'd all be me forever.

74

Boys playing on a lawn
    deciding the rules of football
        how else do boys spend their time
            together & not kill each other?

79

A Chocolate State of Mind

Hot, rolling across the tongue,
swallowed
a momentary high
with afterglow of calm sweet breath.
I dive into thoughtlessness
come up gasping
and write a poem.

71

If I didn't write
I would be nothing

Ars Poetica by Pablo Neruda
translated by Sasha Newborn

Between shadow and space, among young women and
    new dresses,
I am given a heart made single, and sad dreams—
suddenly pale, forehead throbbing,
the widower in mourning, furious through each day of
    life—
Oh, for every clear glass of water which drowsily I drink,
and from every sound which shivering I greet,
I am always absently thirsty, always coldly feverish,
one ear just coming alive, I have an uncentered anguish
as if thieves or ghosts were about to come,
I'm in a huge rigid dome

like a humiliated waiter, like a bell gone sour,
like a chipped mirror, like the smell of a bachelor's house
in which guests arrive at night already wildly drunk,
and which smells of clothes discarded on the floor, and
      no flowers
—possibly there's another way which is even less sad—
but—truth! quickly!—the wind which beats against my
      chest,
the nights of infinite substance tumbling through my
      bedroom,
the clamor of a day which burns with sacrifice
ask me sadly for the prophet in me,
and there is a welter of things which call and are not
      answered,
and a ceaseless restlessness, and a confused man.

76

Nothing human is done for evil.
And in the burning SLA house, who
fires back at police, who
dies by flame, the ammunition
belts around their waists exploded
by the heat? One black, one white
woman. Two or three
men. One hostage escapes from the
equation, now burning.
Burning, too, the determination
not to surrender.
Pride, honesty, will, seeing clearly
the nature of evil
outside, firing in.

73

My first big spiritual revelation,
age eight,
was books.
All of a sudden I could see
with my mind's eye
worlds beyond my street,
my hometown.

Then,
when I walked into
the public library,
I thought to myself—

It'll take me years
to read
all these books.

72

Fire drives out water
from the logs last night's rain
drenched. Did you notice
as you came in, how the clouds,
having wept, shone white?

One red twig curls, lifts, breaks
in that heat. I am waiting for her.

6

Unlacing Lives

She looks like
she's going to speak to us,
he said. He stood in front of
the coffin,
head bent,
nervous,
glancing around finally,
like a big monkey. Papa Human.
And when he turned away from her,
toward us,
his eyes were small and moist,
like mine.
Look, he said, surprised,
it's as if she were going to
get up out of there
and say something.

16

If I were lonely, I'd holler
Dark echoes from an old-as-life wound
Without the flicker of an I,
This habit-bundle hoax of bad decisions.
Across a Russian tablecloth,
Are those your shoulders screaming?
The chaos of myself resurrected,
Morning-shutter sun-eye day,
Relaxes into tensions of being someone else,
A yesterday grown old but not forgotten.
O, to forget and start again.
My hand, here, started once a billion years ago,
The urge, so-called,
A pseudo-extension on a single cell,
Reaching now through this pen and poem,
Reaching…
Someone with my other body needs me.
Hand cease, heart listen.

60

For two days I've been wrestling over
Waterlilies, by Monet.
It came in a box.
Each piece, knobbed or holed,
has just such brush strokes, just so
as to be that place, no other.
And Monet, seventy-plus, sits in his garden
watching waterlilies,
letting those white and pink
flowers pass through his dimmed eyes,
through hands, palette, canvas
(five feet by six)
and the painting survives two wars
in a family attic
to arrive, momentarily
in front of me on the living room floor—
Oh, Monet, you pure clean old man, who saw,
I see the shape of your life,
by looking at Waterlilies, I see.

My lady in a hurry—
you can't change her mind about anything.
She's living in a flurry
of promises and speculation
I hardly see her in the morning,
make her coffee as she races out the door.
When times get tough, she's ready.
She's mean at the machine,
works eight hours steady.
I love her, but the time for love is fleeting
as we struggle up a ladder slipping down.

65

No one chooses to be old,
the gums, the bones, slowing you down,
slowing, stopping at death.

What was it you asked so long ago:
Why is the sky blue?

64

The trouble with reality, I've often said,
is its hardness,
unarguability, obdurate insistent
whining thereness.
Aside from that, I find
the orange juice tart,
toast cold,
and marmalade bitter.
Who could complain?

69

Summer Solstice 1975

Framed in a Volkswagen window,
the Graces smile, honk, are gone.
The women go; I water the garden tonight;
why do I always need to piss
when I hold that hose?
This is the first day of summer; our corn
is finally coming up. Broccoli's been eaten,
the plants composted,
the bed prepared again—today it is naked.
I lay naked in bed today—the window breeze
across my belly
awakens memories of someone else I used to be,
when naked was a thrill, an ecstasy,
before I knew what fucking was.
Take a life, insert poetry.
What is my ritual for the heat of the year? I
hold my cock and squeeze.

61

There's a thing called love
                    we dangle in front of us
waiting for someone to fondle it.
We try to give it away,
but everyone we meet
has that invisible bobble they stare at
in front of them—
when we bump into it, they wince
but try not to yell.

I love every wrinkle on your face
I put them there,
with every careless word
I made your face to be
old, like me.

You can read my wrinkles like a map
of where we've been—
a hieroglyph, a sign for
what I've never said,
what I never will.

66

I have shoved my time aside—
between work and living
—squeezed between sky and earth
    HOLD! Like Atlas, the eternal shove
against the space I stand in.
Is this selfish? Me? Who is talking about me?

63

Taos Brook

What I heard in the brook was silence,
a space between moments
and notes rippling through my head
                              that I caught
in the tangle of strings
laid across my guitar.
A mountain bird crouched on that wet rock,
facing up the stream now grown fat
that eagerly tumbled toward maturity.
The bird saw fish, sang,
and leaped midcoldbrook
under, emerged, fed or not fed
on another rock
upstream; plunged
And again snatched
at the beauty of food,
the folly of slippery feelings
that will not be caught
except by cunning.
As I these notes, this bird
water, trees sunlit
sparkle into melody,
which is not the silence that I heard.

62

Practice while hiking—
sensitivity, odors,
prod with stick, blindfolded
holding one's breath,
walking quietly,
slowing to speed of eternity.

Ghost of Jason walks with me,
teaching me the ways,
the powers, how to
manipulate one's odors.

10

No Way Home

I talked to him last week.
He said, I didn't die,
it's all a mistake.
You know me, don't you?
I'm your Dad.
And last night, again,
there wasn't any question,
not a whisper, no hint
of the last thirty years
of hip replacement, stroke
and mumbled speech,
withering and shrinking,
white hair and spittle.
No, he was re-arranging furniture,
trying to get me to take more stuff
on the trip home,
after the rain would stop.
And I found treasures amid the
attic's offerings, old radios,
harmonicas, bookcases heavy and dark.
He was vigorous, his speech was firm
and warm and clear,
and I wasn't to worry about anything
because he was there.

The coolness of morning shadows
Shivers me to enter into touching,
Green into black, there, the damp areas
Clotted with memory, a catch in the throat of the past.
Musty earth, leaf-littered by the seasons and lilacs,
A room of stalks inside the bush, for wild children
To be caged. Come, summer's calling. Come
To the shades; come with fear and strangeness.

A cloud passing—look, all darkness cancelled
In the compassing gray. Light and dark fused,
Tension lost, a fog, a sea of weather washes smooth
Division. We are all adrift, emotion-lost,
Energy-less, floating down on uncapped time-wave,
Helpless, co-equal, members of a family;
Awaiting rain.

30

Trees Are My Contemporaries

In the woods, the sounds are comforting,
but they make this world seem enormous.
Birds like tin drain pipes,
birds like squealing wheels,
birds like…nothing but birds—
and after the birdsongs ceased
at certain times of day
or going into night,
the echoless woods felt like a church
on a weekday—
that's the closest to the feeling
when I became aware that I had been
listening to the sounds of my own feet,
my own breathing,
and the rhythmic creaking
of the big red pack in its frame on my back,
and I would stop.

Why I Write

Inside, a creature with a stick,
motioning at the bunch of bananas
placed two feet away, too far
for the hands to grasp.
He picks up the stick.
It is black.
He takes the stick apart,
and puts one end on the other end.
Then he writes:

"Dear Sir or Madam:
        Please send me
one (1) bunch of bananas,
please right away.
I'm hungry.
Thank you.

Very truly yours,
Monkey with a stick."

Then he throws the stick down, and
eats the paper.

Do You Believe in God?

I believe that I am flesh,
that the eyes I see with are human eyes,
the understanding that I have is earthly.
If there is a God, I haven't seen him or her or it.

What I have seen and felt is
the wonder of being alive at all,
and moving, in the midst of other living beings.
Time is my treasure. I sense
that that wonder will not stop with my death,
though heart and blood and brain be still.

You lie beside me
under white blankets
turned to the wall.
It was about the diaphragm.
You said ————
And I said —————
which snapped it.

An unborn heaviness
heaps down on us separately,
on you for what I said,
on me for what I didn't know I said.
If this were a foggy night, we'd hear
the foghorn in the harbor
warning ships away from danger.
Right through our bedroom window
that voice of God.
But tonight is too clear for that,
too quiet.

39

She fell. Alert, he turned his head.
"What was that?" I said,
But he was already up, and
Halfway to the door.
He didn't ask, "Are you all right?" He knew.
With clumsy, practiced hands—I saw
On the counter his age-freckled hand
To support him leaning down
Next to hers, strong-veined, getting up—
They accomplished it at length.
She came in, then. "I knocked over
the chocolates," she said.
He said, "Sit here."
She sat, ashamed of being old.
"I knocked them over," she said.
"If you want to move," he said,
"Call me. Please?"
She stared at the table.
"Please, Mummy-love?" he said.
She looked over at me then, pouting.
"The chocolates," she said.

31

When you want to say a thing, spit it out.
Then we can all look at it,
comment on the shape, bubbles, viscosity,
and, in general, its worth.
We may not all agree
whether this particular sputum belongs
on this specific sidewalk.
Someone may smear it on his shoe,
thoughtlessly—
or the sun may sop it up at leisure.
Still, it is indisputably
there, a concrete proposal,
a fluid observation.
You made it.
Now,
what are you going to do about it?

37

Bicycling today, waiting at counters, in lines—
and in the breeze
feeling my sweat   cooling,
the inside of my impatience, the whiff of
my rubber pad under the sheet
to keep the mattress from stinking.
I have been
and am
solely responsible for this act
and all others I may perform.

36

It's winter in Iowa—
I've never been colder than in winter in Iowa,
      snow falling like wet leaves soundlessly,
      wind like whips with diamonds
I've never been colder,
Except now,
Whispering through long-distance at my ear
My father's voice says, of his sister,
"You know, Tood and I are the only ones left out of
      twelve."
He counts them as they go,
Like paratroopers into the beyond.
"Mother's feeling better today—she's sleeping soundly
The sun's shining, but not enough to melt the snow
      away;
I've got a pain in my right leg."
They're dying—winter will do them in.

Year after year the drifts come, bringing cold.
This year horses died,
and cattle, not two counties away,
stood
frozen to the ground.
Geronimo! "You remember Ivan Barnes, who moved in
        across the street some years ago? He's dead."
I can't listen, these words disconnect—
he talks as if they're all waiting for him,
cheering him on.
I say, "Take care...
        of Mother,"
and,
"It's good...talking to you,"
and hang up.

Take off your shoes
as often as possible.
Let your feet breathe.
Poor forgotten cousins
to the hands!
Because our lower hands became feet,
we can walk the Earth.

32

Sleeping Together

Aside from the sex
            —entirely another subject!
sleeping together is a groove.
Warmth to warmth,
in that eerie period of hovering
just above sleep,
that human touching—
can there be anything like it?
I haven't found
any substitute.

3

Music just came to me today—
unbidden but ever inventive.
Few days offer so much
and I had no paper to write it down,
if it could be written down—
that might destroy it.
Today is a day just to be.

12

The Perennial Student

A friend of mine posed
the question:
What do you do
with the rest of your life?

I didn't think much about it
at the time,
passing it off into
Rhetorical Questions that
Don't Call for an Answer.

Today I retrieved it—
something about it stuck to me,
perhaps the annoying thought
that I didn't have a quick glib comeback,
as I do on many repetitive questions,
such as,
Where are you from?

20

I'd be happier if
she didn't just lay on her back
and take it.
Once in a while, she's got more energy
for it than I do,
and she'll climb aboard—
I like that,
like the feeling of being handled,
of being the woman,
because I'm pretty used to the other,
and I want something new.
To be a woman, for me,
is always interesting.

28

The more I read of yogis' stuff,
the more I know that I'm not there.
Such childish grins on those guys,
really happy.
I'm not ready to be happy, or,
let me say, not ready to give up
trying to grab at happiness from
"job-well-done" and "just-rewards" and
sex, can't forget sex—
I can't let it go.

25

Jason, His Tail

I can do New York Times
crossword puzzles,

but I can't cheat death.

(*March 1997*)

24

I left my clothes on a sandbar
off the shore—
the water was still going out,
but I shouldn't be long—
this whole long flat beach
would be covered by the tide again
in the morning—
now only the moon and I
seemed to be alive in this world.
I felt not at the edge but at the very center
of where things happen,
going through the center, holy,
and if there were a god close to that,
and if there weren't,
then I'd be in the place of the absent god,
in the center of love and power.

29

Goddamn, I really do
get a kind of inner cold sweat
looking at blank paper.
Blank? It's never blank.
Even if the writing
purged away my memories,
I have an endless stream.

21

suck out a little at a time,
squeeze the grunts away—
can I be comfortable & civilized
& also ecstatic?

27

It has taken me
this many years
to be able to
put ideas into actions—
and there are still
too many ideas.

26

The principle of democracy
masks an important truth—
valuing other people's minds,
their opinions,
not for their rightness
but for their very existence.
Democracy is the admission that
no one of us can say it all.

23

The Point of Art

Emotion is the point of art.
In great & not-so-great
pieces of art, music, dance, theater
the technique and format
may vary in effectiveness
but
the communication of
complex human feelings
is best expressed in
song
or art
or fiction
—better than in
our own real life.

The manner of art may shift.
Beauty has long since
ceased to be
the primary criterion
for excellence in arts.

22

When I write
in my diary,
it's as if
I'm writing to
myself when younger—
as if
to explain the life lessons
that I learned
the hard way—
by living them.

2

There's always something
to be said,
n'est-ce pas?

Numbers

Congratulations if you've figured
it out. If not, the numbers from
one to one hundred are listed in
alphabetical order, the earliest
being 8 (eight) and the last 2 (two).
Nothing mystical or symbolic
about it.

What's the point? Just another way
of looking at something so
familiar that we forget that our
assumption is just that, an
assumption.

Someone just might
re-arrange the same facts that
you see as obvious, in a way
that you might never have guessed,
if you didn't recognize a different
organizing principle.